T0200980

Copyright © 2024 Uplift Games™
Adopt Me!™
Visit playadopt.me and join the fun!
Ask a parent before going online.

UPLIFT
GAMES

All rights reserved. Manufactured in Malaysia.
No part of this book may be used or reproduced in any manner whatsoever without written permission
except in the case of brief quotations embodied in critical articles and reviews. For information address
HarperCollins Children's Books, a division of HarperCollins Publishers, 195 Broadway, New York, NY 10007.
www.harpercollinschildrens.com

ISBN 978-0-06-331802-1

24 25 26 27 28 COS 10 9 8 7 6 5 4 3 2 1
Originally published in Great Britain 2024 by Farshore
First US edition, 2024

ONLINE SAFETY FOR YOUNGER FANS

Spending time online is great fun! Here are a few simple rules to help younger fans
stay safe and keep the internet a great place to spend time:
- Never give out your real name – don't use it as your username.
- Never give out any of your personal details.
- Never tell anybody which school you go to or how old you are.
- Never tell anybody your password except a parent or a guardian.
- Be aware that you must be 13 or over to create an account on many sites. Always check the site
policy and ask a parent or guardian for permission before registering.
- Always tell a parent or guardian if something is worrying you.

Stay safe online. Any website addresses listed in this book are correct at the time of going to print. However, Farshore is not
responsible for content hosted by third parties. Please be aware that online content can be subject to change and websites
can contain content that is unsuitable for children. We advise that all children are supervised when using the internet.

MIX
Paper | Supporting
responsible forestry
FSC™ C007454

This book contains FSC™ certified paper and other controlled
sources to ensure responsible forest management.

For more information visit: www.harpercollins.co.uk/green

ADOPT ME!

HIDE & SEEK
PETS

HARPER
An Imprint of HarperCollinsPublishers

CONTENTS

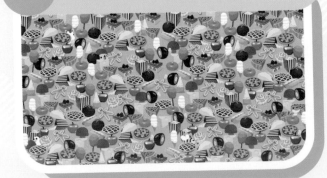

20 POOL PARTY

22 STAR SEARCH

24 SALON SOCIAL

26 PIZZA PARTY

28 HIDE AND SCOOP

30 EGG PARADE

32 HOW TO DRAW

34 MORE TO FIND

ANSWERS ON PAGES 38-39

MEET THE PETS!

Say hello to your new friends. They are eager to start exploring Adoption Island, and while you've been busy setting up your new home, they have all wandered off! Looks like you'll have to go and find them! Where will you look first?

UNICORN

Its rainbow mane is what sets this Legendary pet apart from the crowd. The Unicorn will be a loyal friend, making all your hangouts truly magical. Look for its colorful mane and tail when seeking its hiding place!

BEE

The Bee is a sweet pet pal and will be happy to buzz around Adoption Island with you. This winged wonder loves to explore. Remember to look to the skies when searching for its hiding places.

DOG

This four-legged furry pal will be a fun family friend. This faithful pet will stay by your side on Adoption Island, when it's not running off for a game of hide and seek! Where will you look first for its waggy tail?

T-REX

This roar-some dino friend will be happy to show you all the best places to hang out. Unless it's trying to hide from you, that is! Look out for its toothy grin when you're searching Adoption Island for it!

PENGUIN

This bird is no frosty pal. The Penguin loves to slide on its belly to get around the island, when it's not showing off its moves at the skating rink, of course! How quickly will you spot this black-and-white friend?

NURSERY NEWBIES

Our first stop is the Nursery. Everyone gathers here to collect eggs and welcome new friends. Can you spot your pet pals in the crowd? Better be quick before they move on!

Can you also find:
LEGENDARY PET - Kangaroo

PLAYGROUND PALS

Time to have some fun! The playground is swinging, bouncing, sliding and jumping with pets. How will you ever find your pet friends in this crowd? Try out the fun activities here while you think about where they could be hiding.

Can you also find:
LEGENDARY PET - Crow

POTION COMMOTION

Our intrepid pet friends have found themselves in the Sky Castle. There are magical potions to allow your pet to fly, to travel at hyperspeed and even to grow a big head! Who can you spot hiding among the bottles?

Can you also find:
LEGENDARY PET - Fallow Deer

CAMPSITE CUTIES

Welcome to the great outdoors, a place where pets can take a well-earned rest under canvas or roast a sweet marshmallow over the crackling campfire. Our pet pals are hiding nearby. Can you find them all?

Can you also find:
LEGENDARY PET - Octopus

15

STUDY BUDDIES

There's chaos in the classroom today! There aren't enough desks for all these eager pets. Where are they all going to sit for their lessons? Can you be the teacher's pet and find them all? Class dismissed!

Can you also find:
LEGENDARY PET - Griffin

TASTY TREATS

Ice cream, cakes, pies ... what more could a hungry pet want? Our intrepid friends are hiding in this wonderland of sweet snacks and tasty bites. Don't let your rumbling tummy distract you from finding them all.

Can you also find:
LEGENDARY PET - Dodo

POOL PARTY

Make a splash at the pool and wave to this crowd of pet friends. The search for the pets is going swimmingly well so far! Where will you find them this time? Floating among these cool inflatables, perhaps?

Can you also find:
LEGENDARY PET - Alicorn

STAR SEARCH

Hang out with the star pets at the Celebrity Mansion, but watch out for the paparazzi while you're partying with your pals. Your pets are staying out of the spotlight today. Can you spot where they're hiding?

Can you also find:
LEGENDARY PET - Dragon

SALON SOCIAL

Take some time away from your busy schedule to vist the Salon for some self-care! You can change the color of your pet or even your own hair. Can you spot your pets hiding among these colorful hairsprays and accessories?

Can you also find:
LEGENDARY PET - Axolotl

24

PIZZA PARTY

It's pizza time! Dough not worry—even though the Pizza Shop is busy serving all these customers, you will still be able to find your pet friends. Make sure you leave no pizza unturned until they are all found.

Can you also find:
LEGENDARY PET - Kitsune

HIDE AND SCOOP

Everybody FREEZE! It looks like most of the pets on Adoption Island have arrived at the Ice Cream Shop to sample some tasty frozen treats. Who can you spot enjoying a cone? Don't be frosty and forget to find your pet friends!

Can you also find:
LEGENDARY PET - Giraffe

EGG PARADE

Are you having an egg-cellent time searching for your pet friends? Where are they now? They must be taking shell-ter among these amazing eggs. How long will it take you to find them? Better get cracking!

Can you also find:
LEGENDARY PET - Peacock

HOW TO DRAW
T-REX IN 7 STEPS

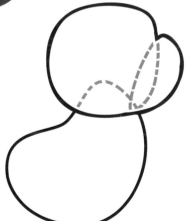

1

Use a pencil to sketch these three basic shapes. Overlap the three shapes to make the head, snout and body. Take your time to get it right.

2

Once you are happy with the shapes, tidy up the lines around the head, snout and body, and erase any messy or overlapped lines.

3

Sketch a pointy tail, a wavy line on the head (to create a mouth) and another to create the tummy of the T-Rex.

4

Now draw the hands and feet. Erase the overlapping line between the tail and body.

5

Add some detail: small circles for the eyes and nostril, scales on the head and tail and claws on the hands and feet.

6

Add a brow line across the top of the eyes, four pointy teeth and some markings along the back and tail. Erase any overlapping lines.

7

Congratulations! You have drawn a T-Rex! Grab your colored pencils and color it in to match the main picture.

MORE TO FIND

Congratulations! Your journey across Adoption Island has been a success, and you managed to find all your pet friends. Can you put your seeking skills to the test once more? Turn back to the beginning and see how many of these other pets you can spot.

NURSERY NEWBIES

- ◯ 2 pets with Ice Cream Cone Hats
- ◯ 2 pets with Orange Glasses
- ◯ 1 pet with Pride Glasses
- ◯ 1 pet with a Leprechaun Hat
- ◯ 2 pets holding slices of Watermelon

PLAYGROUND PALS

- ◯ 1 pet wearing a Bat Backpack
- ◯ 2 pets with an Eco Red Apple Basket Hat
- ◯ 2 pets wearing Umbrella Hats
- ◯ 1 pet wearing a Paw Print Neckerchief
- ◯ 3 pets wearing Pride Headphones

34

CAMPSITE CUTIES

- ○ 1 pet wearing a Bear Winter Hat
- ○ 2 pets wearing Eagle Wings
- ○ 2 pets with Eco Brown Hiking Backpacks
- ○ 1 pet wearing an Eco Red Mushroom Hood
- ○ 2 pets holding Water

STUDY BUDDIES

- ○ 3 pets using RGB Laptops
- ○ 2 pets wearing RGB Headsets
- ○ 4 pets holding Books
- ○ 2 pets holding Water
- ○ 1 pet holding a Healing Apple

POOL PARTY

◯ 1 pet on a blue Mermaid Float

◯ 2 pets on a red Floatie Raft

◯ 2 pets on a pink Pool Noodle

◯ 3 pets holding Star Balloons

◯ 4 pets with pink Ice Creams

STAR SEARCH

◯ 1 pet wearing a Ghost Hat

◯ 3 pets wearing Flower Crowns

◯ 2 pets with Fantastical Wings

◯ 1 pet with Rainbow Cloud Wings

◯ 2 pets wearing Orange Glasses

PIZZA PARTY

- ◯ 1 pet wearing Magpie Wings
- ◯ 3 pets wearing Party Hats
- ◯ 2 pets wearing Knitted Pumpkin Hats
- ◯ 1 pet wearing an RGB Headset
- ◯ 2 pets wearing Headbands

HIDE AND SCOOP

- ◯ 1 pet wearing Cherry Earrings
- ◯ 2 pets wearing Ski Goggles
- ◯ 2 pets wearing Ice Wings
- ◯ 1 pet wearing a Spring Bunny Nose
- ◯ 2 pets wearing Ice Crowns

ANSWERS

KEY:

Main Pets

Legendary Pets

More to Find

8 NURSERY NEWBIES

10 PLAYGROUND PALS

12 POTION COMMOTION

14 CAMPSITE CUTIES

16 STUDY BUDDIES

18 TASTY TREATS

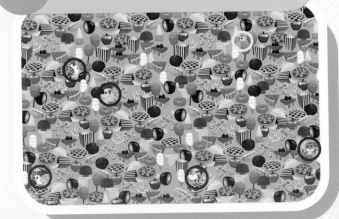

20 POOL PARTY

22 STAR SEARCH

24 SALON SOCIAL

26 PIZZA PARTY

28 HIDE AND SCOOP

30 EGG PARADE